Unit 5

HOUGHTON MIFFLIN HARCOURT
School Publishers

Contents

Mark Shark

by Melissa Rothman
illustrated by Teri Sloat

Mark Shark swam by this harp in
the deep, dark sea. Mark Shark had
never seen a harp. Can he play it?

Mark plucked at a few strings,
and a few notes came out.

He made soft plucks. He plucked
loudly. He played and played.

4

Mark's pals had not seen him in a long time.

"I shall find Mark," said Carl. Off swam Carl.

Carl swam and swam. At last,
sweet tunes filled the sea. Carl swam
to see what made the sweet tunes.

"Mark!" said Carl. "I didn't know you played the harp!"

"I just started and kept playing each day," said Mark.

Carl swam back to tell his pals.
Then they all swam off to see Mark.
Mark played, and the sharks all
sang.

Mark's pals asked Mark to teach them to play.

"It's not that hard," said Mark, "but you must play each day. You must not give up."

Mark was a huge star. Mark and his pals played and sang each day. They filled the sea with sweet tunes.

Clark's Part

by Jay Griffin

illustrated by Adjoa Burrowes

"Mom!" said Clark. "I got a part
in the class show. I will be a big dog
in the show."

"Five kids in dog masks and capes will march on stage and make barking noises. Then we will act out a story," said Clark.

"Let's start to read your part," said Mom. "Let's start."

While Clark rode his bike that
weekend, he said his part. A cat
darted in his way. Clark missed
that cat, but he fell hard on the
park path.

Clark had sharp pain in his arm.
He needed a cast on his arm.

Clark had to start to do things
with his left hand.

His classmates wrote on his cast.

"Can you write?" asked Rick.

"Maybe with my left hand," said Clark.

"I hope you can still play your part," said Nell.

Mom is at the class show. Clark had on his mask and cape.

"Will you know me when I am on stage?" asked Clark.

"I will know your bark," said Mom with a smile.

That night, five kids marched on stage. Clark was not hard to see!

At the Shore

by Jared Chiang

This is the shore. It is where land and sea meet.

You can see sand, grass, and shells on the shore.

Carl's home is on the shore. Carl can see the sea from his window.

Mom, Carl, and Jill go for a short walk. Jill likes to see waves crash on the shore.

Tess is Carl's pal. She hunts for seashells.

Carl sees a crab in its shell. The crab will grow too big for that shell. Then it must find a shell that fits!

Carl and Tess see a few seagulls. More and more seagulls will come. Seagulls hunt for food in the sea and on the shore.

Carl hopes to get a sailboat. Carl will sail far. He will see the world. Then he will head back home and write a story.

More Fun for Jake

by Melissa Rothman

illustrated by John Hovell

Every day Jake's dad runs on
the shore. Dad runs and runs.

Every night, Jake dreams of being like his dad. "When I grow up, I will run like Dad. I will be fast, and I will run far."

One day Jake and his dad went
to a sports store. Jake needed a few
things.

"I like these green shorts and this
red cap," Jake said.

When the weekend came, Dad
asked Jake to run with him. Jake
wore his green shorts and red cap.
Dad and Jake ran and ran.

Each weekend, Jake and Dad ran.
One day, Jake showed Dad a note.
It said, "Race for Dads and Cubs."
Can Dad and Jake race?

"Would you like to be in that race?" Dad asked Jake.

"Yes, yes, yes!" said Jake. "I can be in it."

On the day of the race, Jake
wore his green shorts and his red
cap. Mom came to clap loudly for
Jake and Dad.

The race was fun. Jake didn't
want to stop.

"Let's race!" yelled Jake.

"Yes, we will, but let's wait for the
weekend," said Dad.

See the Birds

by Susie Dietz

Look at this bird perched on a tree branch. She has a sweet song. Chirp, chirp, chirp. She can chirp a happy song.

35

It is fall. The bird that is perched in this tree will find lots to eat. Every time he turns, he will see a treat.

When it turns cold, it is hard to get food. This bird gets food in wet snow.

It is spring. This bird has made
her nest with sticks, wet dirt, and
soft grass. She sits in her nest.

Her eggs will be safe in this nest.
The chicks are curled up inside the
eggs. They will not be hurt.

The first baby bird will burst its
shell. The chick cannot see yet, but it
can peep.

Four baby birds sit in this nest.
They perk up when mom bird brings
food.

This is not a chick. It is a young bird with dark spots. When she is grown up, she will look just like her mom. She will make her own nest and have her own baby birds.

A Bath for Mert

by Maryann Cristensen

illustrated by Lizi Boyd

"Where is Mert?" asked Kate.
Mert was curled up under the porch.
"She is sleeping in the soft dirt,"
said Burt.

43

Mert woke up and jumped to
greet Kate.

Kate turned and said, "Mert has
dirt on her fur. Mert needs a bath."

"Yes," said Burt. "Just follow me.
First, we fill this tub with water. Then
we stir in soap flakes."

Kate and Burt plunked Mert in
the tub. Kate and Burt had to scrub
hard until Mert was clean.

"Hold Mert for me," said Kate.
"Get a firm grip on her, so I can
squirt and take off the suds."

Kate grasped the hose to spray
Mert, but Kate sprayed Burt.

"Stop!" yelled Burt. "You're
squirting me. My shirt is soaked."

Then Mert started to shake,
shake, and shake.

"Stop, Mert," yelled Kate. "Don't
shake so much. My shirt and skirt
are soaked!"

"Mom, we gave Mert the best bath," Burt boasted.

Mert barked and barked.

"Maybe Mert gave you baths, too!" said Mom.

Fox and Crow

retold by Melissa Rothman

illustrated by Tom Sperling

Crow is perched in a birch tree.

She sees some grapes on the ground.

Crow grabs the grapes and goes
back to her perch.

Fox passes by. It seems as if
he has not had a meal in years.
    Fox thinks, "If that bird speaks,
she will drop those grapes."

First Fox asks, "What is your name?"

Crow turns her back.

54

Next Fox asks, "Crow, are you feeling well?"

Crow will not speak. Crow will not stir.

Then Fox tells Crow, "It's sad that a bird as nice as you cannot sing." Crow whirls, and then she blurts, "Sir, I am learning to sing!"

The grapes land in soft dirt.
As Crow sings, Fox eats them up.
Then he smiles, turns, and trots off.

Fox tricked Crow this time, but Crow has learned. Fox will not trick her next time!

Meet Gert

by Carmen Santos

illustrated by John Kurtz

This is my friend Gert. She is eight years old. She is in third grade. I wrote about Gert. Turn the pages and meet Gert.

This is Gert at the beach with
her mom. She begins her day in the
shade. She doesn't want to burn.
She is reading about surfing.

This is Gert with her pictures of
birds chirping. Gert likes to take
pictures of birds perched in trees.
Gert likes red birds. She likes red
the best.

This is Gert on a team. She plays
sports with girls her age. Gert is good
at kicking. She and her teammates
have on red shirts and shorts.

This is Gert on skates. She has
on a green shirt and skirt. Gert
is just learning to turn on one leg.
Gert likes when her skirt spins.

This is Gert at a race. She has
on a white shirt and shorts. Gert is
crossing the red line first. She will
win first prize.

This is Gert in a pink skirt.
She has burst on to the stage and
is whirling and whirling. Gert has
fun whirling.

This is Gert with me. We met in
first grade. Now it is Gert's turn to
write about me!

Look at This!

by Louise Tidd

illustrated by Marilyn Janovitz

"Mom," said Tad, "let's go for a nice bike ride along the path."

Tad and Mom got on this big bike. They took a ride on a bike path.

When Mom and Tad got back
again, Trish was out.

"Let's go and see Trish," said Tad.
"Trish is in her yard."

"What is this?" asked Mom.

"I am planting seeds. Green
bean plants and green pea plants will
grow," said Trish. Then Trish stood up.

69

"Can we plant seeds, Mom?"
asked Tad. "It looks like fun."

"We can, but it is not just fun,"
said Mom. "It is work."

Trish gave them some seeds.

"Growing these plants is fun and work. If you work hard you will get a good prize," said Trish.

Tad and Mom took the seeds
and went home. Tad made holes in
the dirt. Then he put seeds in them.
Mom put dirt over the seeds that
Tad planted.

Tad and Mom had to water their
plants and pull up weeds. Tad and
Mom watched their plants grow big.

"Look!" yelled Tad. "Look at these
big plants!"

"Look at these plants! What can
we do with them?" asked Tad.

"We can eat them," said Mom.

"Such good prizes!" said Tad.

Two Good Cooks

by Gretchen Nguyen

illustrated by Laura Rader

Mom is on her way home. Mom
will be late. My father and I will
cook. We began with a good plan.

We look at this shelf. We see
eggs and ham and cheese and milk.
Those will be good to cook with.

We take out eggs, ham, cheese,
and milk. Then we get bowls and
forks and pans. We can't cook yet.

Dad hands me Mom's cookbook. It will tell us how to cook. We look at the page that shows us how to cook eggs. This is it!

This cookbook tells us to get eggs,
milk, ham, and cheese.

"This looks good!" I say. "We
have eggs, milk, ham, and cheese."

I mix eggs and milk. Dad cuts
ham and cheese into bits. Then I mix
ham and cheese in with the eggs.
Dad will heat the eggs, ham, and
cheese in a pan.

Just then I see Mom.

"That smells so good! What is it?" she asks. "Can I look?"

"Just sit and we will bring it to you," I say. "Then you can look."

Mom laughs and sits.
"This is a real treat. You and
Dad did a good deed!" said Mom.

Good Homes

by Louise Tidd

These insects are bees.
Can you hear them buzz?

Bees live together in hives.
Hives are good homes for bees.

Each hive has a queen. The queen bee does nothing but lay eggs. That is her job. These bees feed their queen bee.

Caves make good homes for bats. Bats sleep all day. They hook their back feet in cracks. Bats sleep upside down.

It is dark when bats wake up.
Bats hear much better than they
can see. Bats make squeaks to tell
if it is safe.

This cute fellow is a rabbit. Rabbits dig burrows. A burrow is a big hole.

If one rabbit sees a problem, it
thumps its foot. Then the rabbits
run back in their burrow to be safe.

Hives, caves, and burrows make good animal homes. This is not an animal home. It is for kids. Can you tell what it is?

Big Problems

by Jackson Prescott

illustrated by Shari Halpern

Ray is a boy. He has a dog.
Ray's dog is Dennis. Dennis had
problems that began when he was
just a pup.

Dennis was much too big to fit in his dog bed. It was a problem.

"Dennis needs a big bed," said Ray. "Yes, Dennis needs a big bed."

Ray gave Dennis big soft yellow pillows. Did Dennis like his yellow bed? Dennis did. It was nice and soft. Better yet, it was big.

As Dennis got big, his problems got big as well. It was hard for Ray to take Dennis for a walk.

"This is a problem," said Ray. "It is a big problem."

So, Ray began to ride on, not
walk with, Dennis. Did Dennis like
this? Dennis did. Did Ray like this?
Ray did like it. Dad did, too.
    "No problem," said Ray.

As Dennis got big, so did his problems. When Dennis stood up, he did not fit in his dog house.

"You need a big house," said Ray.

"We can make a big house for Dennis," said Dad.

So Ray, his sister, and his dad made a big house for Dennis.

Dennis and Ray can fit in the big
house. Dennis likes that. Ray likes
it, too. Dennis and Ray like to be
together.

"No problems," said Ray.

Moose's Tooth

by Paul Giuliano
illustrated by Sachiko Yoshikawa

Moose has a loose tooth. His
loose tooth feels funny. A loose
tooth can go back and forth.

Moose likes to eat water plants. Moose has to get in deep water up to his knees.

Moose dips down and scoops up
all kinds of plants. Moose's food is
wet. Dip and scoop! Dip and scoop!

Moose has a loose tooth. Now,
Moose can't chew his food. Chewing
can make his tooth too loose. Moose
must get a new plan.

Moose has a new plan. Moose takes his food inside. He knows just what to do. If Moose can't chew, he will mix a brew. That is his plan.

Moose adds plants and a spice or two to the mix. His plant and spice mix looks like thick green goop.

Moose adds milk. His green goop
shake is ready. Moose can drink it.
Moose has no need to chew!

Moose likes his new brew.
Moose's loose tooth likes it, too.

Moon News

by James Franklin

This is our moon. We can see the moon at night. We cannot see it at noon. That's a scoop! No moon at noon.

This is a full moon. It can look white. It can look yellow. It can look almost red. The moon is covered with dust and rocks.

This is a new moon. It looks like
a slice of moon. But it is not a moon
slice. A new moon shows just the
part that is lit up.

This moon chart shows ways the moon can look from Earth. It starts with the new moon on day 1. It shows the full moon on day 14.

Look at this painting. It shows
the moon and stars. Did the person
who painted this have fun with the
moon? How can you tell?

This painting shows the moon.
This painting shows what the moon
shone on. It shone on land. It
shone on trees. Trees gleam in the
moon's glow.

This painting shows the moon.
This painting shows what the moon
shone on. It shone on water. Water
gleams in the moon's glow.

Moon Song

I like to look at the moon
and hope to visit it soon.
You can come, too.
You can be in my crew!

Boot's Clues

by Cindy Detmar
illustrated by
Bill Brandon

Here is a tale about Boot and
Sue. I hope you like it! This tale
is just for you.

Drew had to take a trip to the country. He left Boot with Sue.

"Thanks," Drew said. "Boot's clues will tell you what to do."

Boot ran and ran. He picked up
a stick and gave it to Sue.

"Is this a clue?" asked Sue.
"What kind of clue is this, Boot?"

Boot gave Sue a grin.

Sue threw the stick. Boot jumped up.

"He got it! It's a clue!" yelled Sue.

Sue and Boot went inside.
Boot bumped his food bowl
with his nose.

"Is this a clue?" asked Sue.

"That is a neat clue, Boot!" said
Sue. "You let me know that you need
food and water."

Then Sue gave a clue. She turned
off the light to see if Boot would
jump in his bed. Did he do it?

"You did it, Boot!" said
Sue. "You are cute. You give
clues and you get clues!"

Red Zed and Blue Stu

by Kate Pistone
illustrated by Paulette Bogan

Red Zed is a mule. Blue Stu is a
mule. Red Zed and Blue Stu live on
the same hill. The hill is covered with
grass for them to eat.

One day, cool winds blew.

"Blue Stu, it is too cool on this
hill," said Red Zed.

Blue Stu did not say a thing. He
just ate grass.

"Let's look for a new home," Red
Zed went on.

"Let me chew this last bit of
grass. I will be ready at noon," said
Blue Stu. "I need a few more chews."

Blue Stu and Red Zed left the hill.

They got in this crude boat.

Blue Stu rowed and rowed.

"Land ho!" yelled Red Zed. "Land ho! Land ho!"

"I hope there is grass," grunted Blue Stu.

"It is warm on this dune," said Red Zed.

"Yes, but I need food," said Blue Stu. "Let's look for grass."

"Yes, yes," said Red Zed. "Let's!"

The dune was covered with sand,
not soil. No grass could grow on it.

"I need food, too," said Red Zed.
"I need food to eat."

"Let's go back to our cool hill,"
said Blue Stu. He had a plan.

Now, Red Zed and Blue Stu were warm and full. They did not say a thing. They just ate grass.

Down on the Farm

by Siri Hansen

It is spring on this farm. Come
and see a farm animal here.

Up on a hill is a brown horse with white feet. Her foal is with her. Her foal is growing up now.

Out in the grass is a brown and
white cow with her brown and white
baby. Her baby is growing up now.

This cute wood mouse skips along the ground. This mouse likes to sneak into the barn. It likes to get bits of food in the barn.

A barn owl sits in this barn. If
the mouse sees the barn owl, the
mouse will not go in. Barn owls help
keep mice out of barns.

Look at this proud mother pig and her family. She sniffs the ground with her snout. Soon her seven piglets will be as big as their mom.

The wool coat on this mother
sheep is thick and soft! She is with
her lamb. Soon her lamb will have a
thick, soft coat, too.

This hen is with her baby chicks.
Her family stays with her for now.

It's spring down on the farm. It
is time to shout, "Come and see each
animal and its family!"

Scout and Count

by Tawana Ross

illustrated by Philomena O'Neill

Scout sat on the couch when Dad
came into the house. In his arms was
a sweet brown and white pup.

"Miss Crown gave us this pup.
Will we keep him, Scout?"

"Wow!" said Scout. "Yes! Please,
let's keep him. He's so cute. He's a
sweet pup."

"What will we name him?" asked
Dad. "How about Sprout?"

Scout frowned. Then she asked,
"Can we name him Count?"

"Count is a good name," said Dad.

"Here, Count," Scout shouted as Count sniffed around his new house. Count did not come.

"I will teach Count myself," vowed Scout. "It will be like dog school!"

Scout found a bowl for food.

"Here, Count," shouted Scout.

Count did not come. So Scout took that bowl to Count and fed him. Count ate and ate.

Scout found a brush for Count's coat. Scout did not see Count.

"Here, Count," shouted Scout.

Count did not come to her. So Scout found Count, sat down, and brushed his coat.

One day, Scout played out in the yard. Count sat with Dad. Count and Dad sat on the deck.

"Here, Count," shouted Scout. Count jumped down off the deck and ran to Scout.

"Wow! Count knows his name now!" shouted Scout.

"Bow wow," barked Count.

Dawn's Voice

by Eileen Brady
illustrated by Tim Bowers

Dawn had a nice voice.
Outside, her voice was loud.
Inside, her voice was soft.

At times, Dawn forgot which
voice to use. If she forgot at home,
Mom would say, "Use an inside
voice, Dawn."

If she forgot at school, Miss Law
would whisper, "Too much noise.
How can we read? Use an inside
voice, Dawn."

Last week, Dawn was at a school game. Her school's Red Team led the game. The Yellow Team was at bat. The batter swung and hit hard.

Dawn shouted to Paul, "Look up, Paul! Look up!"

Dawn's loud voice filled the park. Would Paul hear it?

Paul did hear it. He looked up
and made the catch. Dawn's team
got the win.

With joy, Dawn joined the school party. Paul thanked Dawn.

"My loud voice was just right!" Dawn shouted. Then she said with her soft voice, "Just right."

Shawn's Toys

by Eileen Brady

illustrated by Steven Parton

Each day Shawn put coins in his
big plastic jar. Shawn would be glad
when his coins filled the jar. Soon
Shawn could buy a new toy.

At night, Shawn dreamed about toys. In his dreams, he saw rows and rows of toys. He had dream toys.

One day, Shawn put five coins in
his jar. "It's full," yelled Shawn.
No more coins would fit.

Shawn dumped his coins. Dad joined Shawn as he counted his coins.

"Let's go to City Toys now. Do you know just what you will get?" asked Dad.

"No, but I will know it when I see it," said Shawn.

Dad and Shawn entered City Toys.
Shawn saw rows of toys, just like in
his dreams.

Roy showed them toys. He
pointed to toy trains that could
haul loads.

Shawn saw trains, trains, trains.

Then Roy pointed at a toy boat.
"This boat can be launched in a
pond," said Roy. "It's so much fun.
You will like this toy."

Shawn saw a brown stuffed toy
with black paws. He pointed at it.
"Please," shouted Shawn. "This is
it! I will buy this toy."

"This toy is the best for me," said Shawn. "It is the best!"

"Good choice," said Dad. "Good choice, Shawn. We will get that."

Word Lists

Mark Shark

page 3

Decodable Words
Target Skill: *r*-Controlled Vowel *ar*
Carl, dark, hard, harp, Mark, Mark's, Shark, sharks, star, started

Previously Taught Skills
and, asked, at, back, but, came, can, day, deep, didn't, each, filled, had, he, him, his, huge, in, it, it's, just, kept, know, last, long, made, must, not, notes, off, pals, play, played, playing, plucked, plucks, sang, sea, see, seen, soft, strings, swam, sweet, teach, tell, that, them, then, this, time, tunes, up, with

High-Frequency Words
New
few, loudly, shall

Previously Taught
a, all, by, find, give, I, never, out, said, the, they, to, was, what, you

163

Clark's Part

Decodable Words

Target Skill: *r*-Controlled Vowel *ar*
arm, bark, barking, Clark, Clark's,
darted, hard, march, marched, park,
part, sharp, start

Previously Taught Skills
act, am, and, asked, at, be, big, bike,
but, can, cape, capes, cast, cat, class,
classmates, do, dog, fell, five, got, had,
hand, he, his, hope, in, is, kids, know,
left, let's, make, mask, masks, maybe,
me, missed, Mom, needed, Nell, not,
on, pain, path, play, read, Rick, rode,
said, see, show, smile, stage, still, that,
then, things, way, we, weekend, when,
while, will, with, write, wrote

High-Frequency Words

New
night, noises, story

Previously Taught
a, I, my, out, the, to, was,
you, your

164

Accompanies *"The Garden"*

At the Shore
page 19

Decodable Words
Target Skill: *r*-Controlled Vowels *or, ore*
for, more, shore, short

Target Skill: *r*-Controlled Vowel *ar*
Carl, Carl's, far

Previously Taught Skills
and, back, big, can, crab, crash, fits,
food, get, go, grass, grow, he, head, his,
home, hopes, hunt, hunts, in, is, it, its,
Jill, land, likes, meet, Mom, must, on,
pal, sail, sailboat, sand, sea, seagulls,
seashells, see, sees, she, shell, shells,
Tess, that, then, this, waves, will, write

High-Frequency Words
New
few, story, window, world

Previously Taught
a, come, find, from, the, to,
too, walk, where, you

More Fun for Jake
page 27

Decodable Words
Target Skill: *r*-Controlled Vowels *or, ore*
for, shore, shorts, sports, store, wore

Target Skill: *r*-Controlled Vowel *ar*
far

Previously Taught Skills
and, asked, be, being, but, came, can, cap,
clap, Cubs, Dad, Dads, day, didn't, dreams,
each, fast, in, fun, green, grow, him, his,
it, Jake, Jake's, let's, like, Mom, needed,
note, on, race, ran, red, run, runs, showed,
stop, that, these, things, this, up, wait, we,
weekend, went, when, will, with, yelled, yes

High-Frequency Words
New
few, loudly, night

Previously Taught
a, every, I, of, one, said,
the, to, want, was,
would, you

See the Birds

page 35

Decodable Words

Target Skill: *r*-Controlled Vowels *er*, *ir*, *ur*

bird, birds, burst, chirp, curled, dirt, first, her, hurt, perched, perk, turns

Previously Taught Skills

and, at, be, branch, brings, but, can, cannot, chick, chicks, dark, eat, eggs, get, gets, grass, grown, hard, has, he, in, inside, is, it, its, just, like, lots, made, make, mom, nest, not, on, own, peep, safe, see, she, shell, sit, sits, snow, soft, song, spots, spring, sticks, sweet, that, this, time, treat, tree, up, wet, when, will, with, yet

High-Frequency Words

New

baby, young

Previously Taught

a, are, cold, every, fall, find, food, four, happy, have, look, the, they, to

166

A Bath for Mert

page 43

Decodable Words
Target Skill: *r*-Controlled Vowels *er*, *ir*, *ur*

Burt, curled, dirt, firm, first, fur, her, Mert, shirt, skirt, squirt, squirting, stir, turned

Previously Taught Skills
and, asked, barked, bath, baths, best, boasted, but, can, clean, fill, flakes, for, gave, get, grasped, greet, grip, had, hard, has, hose, in, is, jumped, just, Kate, maybe, me, Mom, much, needs, off, on, plunked, porch, scrub, shake, she, sleeping, so, soaked, soap, soft, spray, sprayed, started, stop, suds, take, then, this, tub, up, we, with, woke, yelled, yes

High-Frequency Words
New
follow, until

Previously Taught
a, are, don't, hold, I, my, said, the, to, too, under, was, water, where, you, you're

Fox and Crow

page 51

Decodable Words
Target Skill: *r*-Controlled Vowels *er, ir, ur*

birch, bird, blurts, dirt, first, her, perch, perched, sir, stir, turns, whirls

Previously Taught Skills
am, and, as, asks, back, but, cannot, Crow, drop, eats, feeling, Fox, grabs, grapes, had, has, he, if, in, is, it, it's, land, meal, name, next, nice, not, off, on, passes, sad, seems, sees, she, sing, sings, smiles, soft, speak, speaks, tells, that, them, then, thinks, this, those, time, tree, trick, tricked, trots, up, well, will

High-Frequency Words
New
learned, learning, years

Previously Taught
a, are, by, goes, ground, I, some, the, to, what, you, your

Meet Gert

page 59

Decodable Words
Target Skill: *r*-Controlled Vowels *er, ir, ur*

birds, burn, burst, chirping, first, Gert, Gert's, girls, her, perched, shirts, skirt, surfing, third, turn, whirling

Previously Taught Skills
age, and, at, beach, best, crossing, day, fun, grade, green, has, in, is, it, just, kicking, leg, likes, line, me, meet, met, mom, on, pages, pink, plays, prize, race, reading, red, shade, she, shorts, skates, spins, sports, stage, take, team, teammates, this, trees, we, when, white, will, win, with, write, wrote

High-Frequency Words
New
begins, eight, learning, years

Previously Taught
a, about, doesn't, friend, good, have, I, my, now, of, old, one, pictures, the, to, want

168

Look at This!

Decodable Words
Target Skill: Vowel Digraph *oo*
good, look, looks, stood, took

Previously Taught Skills
am, and, asked, at, back, bean, big,
bike, but, can, dirt, eat, for, fun, gave,
get, go, got, green, grow, growing, had,
hard, he, her, holes, home, if, in, is, it,
just, let's, like, made, Mom, nice, not,
on, path, pea, plant, planted, planting,
plants, prize, prizes, ride, see, seeds,
such, Tad, that, them, then, these, this,
Trish, up, we, weeds, went, when, will,
with, yard, yelled

High-Frequency Words
New
again, along

Previously Taught
a, do, I, out, over, pull, put,
said, some, the, their, they,
to, was, watched, water,
what, work, you

Two Good Cooks

page 75

Decodable Words
Target Skill: Vowel Digraph *oo*
cook, cookbook, good, look, looks

Previously Taught Skills
and, asks, at, be, bits, bowls, bring,
can, can't, cheese, cuts, Dad, deed, did,
eggs, forks, get, ham, hands, heat, her,
home, in, is, it, just, late, me, milk, mix,
Mom, Mom's, on, page, pan, pans,
plan, real, say, see, she, shelf, shows,
sit, sits, smells, so, take, tell, tells, that,
then, this, those, treat, us, way, we,
will, with, yet

High-Frequency Words
New
began, father

Previously Taught
a, have, how, I, into, laughs,
my, out, said, the, to, what,
you

Accompanies
"Whistle for Willie"

Good Homes

page 83

Decodable Words
Target Skill: Syllable Pattern (CVC)
better, burrow, burrows, fellow, insects, problem, rabbit, rabbits

Target Skill: Vowel Digraph *oo*
foot, good, hook

Previously Taught Skills
an, and, back, bats, be, bee, bees, big, but, buzz, can, caves, cracks, cute, dark, day, dig, each, eggs, feed, feet, for, has, her, hive, hives, hole, home, homes, if, in, is, it, its, job, kids, lay, make, much, not, queen, run, safe, see, sees, sleep, squeaks, tell, than, that, them, then, these, this, thumps, up, upside, wake, when

High-Frequency Words
New
nothing, together

Previously Taught
a, all, animal, are, does, down, hear, live, one, the, their, they, to, what, you

Big Problems

page 91

Decodable Words
Target Skill: Syllable Pattern (CVC)
better, Dennis, pillows, problem, problems, sister, yellow

Target Skill: Vowel Digraph *oo*
stood

Previously Taught Skills
and, as, be, bed, big, can, Dad, did, dog, fit, for, gave, got, had, hard, has, he, his, in, is, it, just, like, likes, made, make, much, need, needs, nice, no, not, on, pup, Ray, Ray's, ride, so, soft, take, that, this, up, we, well, when, with, yes, yet

High-Frequency Words
New
began, boy, house, together

Previously Taught
a, said, the, to, too, walk, was, you

171

Accompanies
"A Tree is a Plant"

Moose's Tooth

page 99

Decodable Words
Target Skill: Words with *oo, ou, ew*
brew, chew, chewing, food, goop,
loose, Moose, Moose's, new, scoop,
scoops, too, tooth

Previously Taught Skills
adds, and, back, can, can't, deep, dip,
dips, drink, eat, feels, forth, get, go,
green, has, he, his, if, in, inside, is, it,
just, knees, knows, like, likes, looks,
make, milk, mix, must, need, no, or,
plan, plant, plants, shake, spice, takes,
that, thick, up, wet, will

High-Frequency Words
New
kinds, ready

Previously Taught
a, all, do, down, funny, now,
of, the, to, two, water, what

172

Moon News

page 107

Decodable Words

Target Skill: Words with *oo, ou, ew*
crew, moon, moon's, new, noon, scoop,
soon, too, you

Previously Taught Skills
1, 14, and, at, be, but, can, cannot, chart,
day, did, dust, from, fun, gleam, gleams,
glow, hope, in, is, it, just, land, like, lit, look,
looks, no, not, on, painted, painting, part,
person, red, rocks, see, shone, shows, slice,
Song, stars, starts, tell, that, that's, this,
trees, up, visit, ways, we, white, with, yellow

High-Frequency Words

New
almost, covered, Earth

Previously Taught
a, come, full, have, how,
I, my, night, of, our, the,
to, water, what, who

Boot's Clues

page 115

Decodable Words
Target Skill: Words with *ue, u, u_e*
clue, clues, cute, Sue

Target Skill: Words with *oo, ou, ew*
Boot, Boot's, Drew, food, threw, you

Previously Taught Skills
and, asked, bed, bowl, bumped, did,
for, gave, get, got, grin, had, he, his,
hope, if, in, inside, is, it, it's, jump,
jumped, just, know, left, let, like, me,
neat, need, nose, off, picked, ran, see,
she, stick, take, tale, tell, thanks, that,
then, this, trip, turned, up, went, will,
with, yelled

High-Frequency Words
New
country, kind

Previously Taught
a, about, are, do, give, here,
I, light, of, said, the, to,
water, what, would

Red Zed and Blue Stu

page 123

Decodable Words
Target Skill: Words with *ue, u, u_e*
Blue, crude, dune, mule, Stu

Target Skill: Words with *oo, ou, ew*
blew, chew, chews, cool, few, food,
new, noon, too

Previously Taught Skills
and, at, ate, back, be, bit, boat, but,
day, did, eat, for, go, got, grass, grow,
grunted, had, he, hill, ho, home, hope,
in, is, it, just, land, last, left, let, let's,
look, me, more, need, no, not, of, on,
plan, Red, rowed, same, sand, say,
them, thing, this, went, will, winds,
with, yelled, yes, Zed

High-Frequency Words
New
covered, ready, soil, warm

Previously Taught
a, could, full, I, live, now,
one, our, said, the, there,
they, to, was, were

Accompanies
"The New Friend"

Down on the Farm

page 131

Decodable Words
Target Skill: Words with *ou, ow*
brown, cow, down, ground, mouse, now, out, owl, owls, proud, shout, snout

Previously Taught Skills
and, as, at, barn, barns, be, big, bits, chicks, coat, cute, each, farm, feet, foal, food, for, get, go, grass, growing, help, hen, her, hill, horse, if, in, is, it, its, it's, keep, lamb, likes, look, mice, mom, not, on, pig, piglets, see, sees, she, sheep, sits, skips, sneak, sniffs, soft, soon, spring, stays, thick, this, time, too, up, white, will, with, wood, wool

High-Frequency Words
New
family, seven

Previously Taught
a, along, animal, baby, come, have, here, into, mother, of, the, their, to

Scout and Count

page 139

Decodable Words

Target Skill: Words with *ou, ow*

bow, brown, couch, Count, Count's, Crown, down, found, frowned, house, how, now, out, Scout, shouted, Sprout, vowed, wow

Previously Taught Skills

and, arms, as, asked, ate, barked, be, bowl, brush, brushed, came, can, coat, cute, Dad, day, deck, did, dog, fed, food, for, gave, good, he's, her, him, his, in, is, it, jumped, keep, knows, let's, like, Miss, name, new, not, off, on, played, please, pup, ran, sat, see, she, sniffed, so, sweet, teach, that, then, this, took, us, we, when, white, will, with, yard, yes

High-Frequency Words

New

myself, please, school

Previously Taught

a, about, around, come, here, I, into, one, said, the, to, was, what

Dawn's Voice

page 147

Decodable Words
Target Skill: Words with *oi, oy, au, aw*
Dawn, Dawn's, joined, joy, Law, noise, Paul, voice

Target Skill: Words with *ou, ow*
how, loud, outside, shouted

Previously Taught Skills
an, and, at, bat, batter, can, catch, did, filled, forgot, game, got, had, hard, he, her, hit, home, if, inside, it, just, last, led, look, looked, made, Miss, Mom, much, nice, park, read, Red, say, she, soft, swung, team, thanked, then, times, too, up, use, we, week, which, whisper, win, with, Yellow

High-Frequency Words
New
party, school, school's

Previously Taught
a, hear, my, right, said, the, to, was, would

Shawn's Toys

page 155

Decodable Words
Target Skill: Words with *oi, oy, au, aw*
choice, coins, haul, joined, launched, paws, pointed, Roy, saw, Shawn, toy, toys

Target Skill: Words with *ou, ow*
brown, counted, now, shouted

Previously Taught Skills
and, as, asked, at, be, best, big, black, boat, but, can, Dad, day, dream, dreamed, dreams, dumped, each, entered, filled, fit, five, for, fun, get, glad, go, good, had, he, his, in, is, it, it's, jar, just, know, let's, like, loads, me, more, much, new, no, plastic, please, pond, rows, see, showed, so, soon, stuffed, that, them, then, this, trains, we, when, will, with, yelled, you

High-Frequency Words
New
buy, city, please

Previously Taught
a, about, could, do, full, I, night, of, one, put, said, the, to, what, would